Written by C.J. McDonald and Kris Hirschmann
Illustrated and designed by Kristen Pauline

an imprint of

SCHOLASTIC
scholastic.com

Copyright © 2019 Scholastic Inc.
Published by Tangerine Press, an imprint of Scholastic Inc.
557 Broadway
New York, NY 10012

Scholastic UK Ltd.
Westfield Road
Southam
Warwickshire CV47 0RA

10 9 8 7 6 5 4 3 2 1
ISBN: 978-1-338-34898-9
Printed in New Taipei City, Taiwan
Light-up cover made in Shantou, China

Cover designer: Flora Chan
Photo editor: Cynthia Carris

TABLE OF CONTENTS

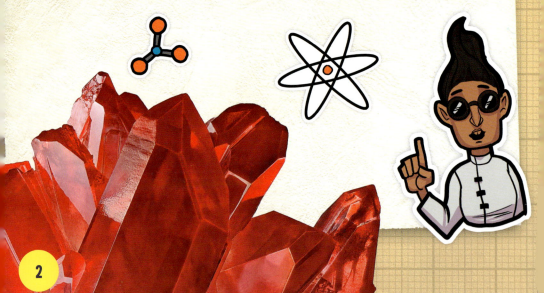

IT'S TIME FOR SOME
COLOSSAL FUN!

Crystals are some of nature's greatest marvels. They're not alive, but they grow, and some have freaky, almost magical powers—things like glowing, making electricity, carrying sound, changing color, or powering electronics. We eat them, we wear them, we sit on them, we drive in them, and our bodies even contain them.

Crystals are solid substances in which **atoms** and **molecules** combine to create repeating **geometric** patterns such as triangles, squares, or rectangles. They contain so many of these tiny shapes that it would take you tens of thousands of years to count them.

They grow with the right combination of time, space, pressure, and heat. The more raw material—salt, sugar, eggshells, or our colossal crystal **solution**—combined with the right timing and conditions, the more colossal results you will get. And we're going to meet some really COLOSSAL crystals found in nature.

WHAT YOU GET IN YOUR KIT:

• 2 packets of crystal-growing powder
• plaster crystal seed
• light-up cover
• plastic measuring cup
• 24-page book with crystal-growing experiments

LET'S MAKE THIS
CRYSTAL CLEAR

Most **minerals** have crystal structures, as do some gems. Crystals form when atoms found within liquid gather together and harden as the liquid cools or **evaporates**. This is called **crystallization**. You'll get to witness how crystals form firsthand in each of your colossal experiments! The slower the liquid cools or evaporates, the larger the crystal.

EACH CRYSTAL HAS ITS OWN UNIQUE COMBINATION OF FOUR CHARACTERISTICS:

SHAPE

The shapes of crystals—known as their **habits**—can be tree-like, square, in clusters, in cylinders, round, or a variety of other shapes.

VANADINITE

AMETHYST

COLOR

You can find crystals in a rainbow of colors. They get their colors from the **elements** within them. Iron gives amethyst crystals their famous purple color, and lead makes vanadinite red.

TRANSPARENCY

Crystals can be **opaque, translucent**, or **transparent**. The more light that can pass through a crystal, the more transparent it is.

CHALCEDONY
(translucent)

QUARTZ
(transparent)

SCHORL TOURMALINE
(opaque)

SIZE

Crystals come in all sizes. They can be so small that they can only be seen under a microscope, or they can also be so big that they tower over you.

SOME COLOSSALLY MIND-BLOWING FACTS:

- **Geodes** are plain-looking rocks with beautiful crystals hiding inside. But they have been known to hide other surprises—like living frogs!

- Your skeleton is made of crystals. You can chew your food because of crystals in your teeth. Weirder yet, crystals in your brain create electricity!

- Scientists have found crystals from space!

- The world's most expensive crystal—the Pink Star diamond—sold for $71 million in 2017!

BEFORE WE BEGIN

Now that you're learning more about how cool crystals are, you're probably ready to grow your own. But not so fast. First take a few minutes to get up to speed on some rules and first-aid tips. Read these instructions before use, follow them and keep for reference.

SAFETY MATTERS!

DID YOU ASK FOR HELP?

- Keep the activity area clean and away from food storage.
- Work in a well-lit, ventilated room with running water.
- Clean the activity area immediately after performing each experiment.
- Wash your hands and clean all equipment after each experiment.
- Use only the materials that are supplied with the kit or recommended in the book in your experiments.
- Do not eat or drink in the activity area.
- Do not grow crystals where food or drink is handled or in bedroom.
- Do not eat or drink the results of the experiments unless the book says you can.
- Contains some chemicals which present a hazard to health.
- Do not allow chemicals to come into contact with any part of the body, particularly the mouth and eyes.
- Some experiments will require you to use common household objects. Ask your adult helper for permission before you use any of these items.
- Keep small children and animals away from experiments.
- Keep and store this experimental set and final crystals out of reach of children under 8 years of age.
- Take care while handling hot water and hot solutions.
- Ensure that during growing of the crystal the container with the liquid is out of reach of children under 8 years of age.

ALWAYS HAVE AN ADULT HELPER AVAILABLE!

WARNINGS ABOUT THE POWDERS:

- Do not inhale dust or powder.
- Do not apply any substances or solutions to the body.
- Avoid contact with eyes. In case of contact with eyes, rinse with plenty of water and seek immediate medical advice.
- If you swallow or have an allergic reaction to the powder, seek medical advice right away. Take the product and package with you.
- The powder may stick, making it difficult to remove. Avoid contact with hair, carpets, and fabric.
- Do not put the powder or the items made with the powders down the drain. Put the powders and items into a plastic bag, seal the bag, and then throw the bag into the trash.
- Ensure that all empty containers and/or non-reclosable packaging are disposed of properly.
- Store the powder in a well-ventilated place.
- Avoid direct exposure to sunlight.
- Do not use the powder in a windy area.

PLEASE ADD TELEPHONE NUMBER OF YOUR LOCAL POISON CONTROL OR HOSPITAL:

SCHOLASTIC CUSTOMER SERVICE:
212-343-6100

✔ DOS...

Do you know people (maybe even you?) who get a little difficult when they don't get their way? Well, crystals are a bit like that. If you don't follow the instructions to the letter or you forget a step, your crystals may not grow at all. Here's how to ensure success:

- ✔ · Have an adult helper with you.
- ✔ · Follow the instructions carefully. Do the steps in order, and remember to use all ingredients.
- ✔ · Make sure your measurements are exact.
- ✔ · Label each experiment with the time and date you started. That will help you track your crystal's progress and tell you when you need to take the next step.
- ✔ · Be patient! Growing crystals can take a long time—sometimes even longer than the time shown in the instructions.

Your crystals may grow bigger or smaller depending upon where you live. Temperature, humidity, or even elevation (living in the mountains vs. in a valley) can affect your results. In a home environment, we can't control pressure, which is one of the four things that determine just how big a crystal will grow.

NOTE TO PARENTS

- Read and follow these instructions, the safety rules and the first aid information, and keep them for reference.
- The incorrect use of chemicals can cause injury and damage to health. Only carry out those experiments which are listed in the instructions.
- This experimental set is for use only by children over 8 years.
- The supervising adult should discuss the warnings and safety information with the child or children before commencing the experiments. Particular attention should be paid to the safe handling of acids, alkalis and flammable liquids.
- The area surrounding the experiment should be kept clear of any obstructions and away from the storage of food. It should be well lit and ventilated and close to a water supply. A solid table with a heat resistant top should be provided.

AND DON'TS

Just as there are several things you need to do to get the most colossal results possible, here are a few things not to do:

- • **DO NOT** disturb your experiments when they are in progress unless instructed. Remember, crystals are temperamental!

- • **DO NOT** place your experiments in direct sunlight, unless the instructions say otherwise.

- • **DO NOT** give up too soon! Your crystals may need more time to grow than the time recommended in this book. When it comes to growing crystals, you should always expect the unexpected!

GREAT SCIENTISTS LEARN FROM MISTAKES!

"I didn't fail 1,000 times. The light bulb was an invention with 1,000 steps."

– INVENTOR THOMAS EDISON

HERE'S A TIP!

If your experiment fails even though you've been really patient waiting for results, try repeating the experiment using a little more solution, and give it a little more time.

COLOSSAL EXPERIMENT 1:
ICE SPIKES

It's finally time to get growing! Let's start with an easy experiment that will give you quick and really cool results.

CRYSTAL GROWTH METER

TIME UNTIL:
VISIBLE CHANGES: TWO HOURS
FINAL RESULTS: FOUR HOURS

WHAT YOU'LL NEED:

* ICE CUBE TRAY
* DISTILLED WATER
* FREEZER

WHAT YOU'LL DO

1. Thoroughly wash, rinse, and dry the ice cube tray.

2. Fill all the basins of the tray with distilled water.

3. Put the tray in the freezer.

4. After four hours, you should see crystal spikes jutting out from some of the ice cubes.

WHY IT WORKS

The edges of ice cubes always freeze first. As the cube freezes from the outside in, ice crystals squeeze the water in the middle. The squeezed water bulges upward, forming spikes—if we follow instructions, that is. It's important to use distilled water and a really clean tray to avoid tiny particles that could prevent ice spikes from growing. If you don't believe us, try using regular water, and compare your results!

NATURAL WONDERS

If you want to see ice spikes gone wild, check out the naturally occurring ones found in South American mountains. They can grow up to 16 ft. (4.9 m) tall! They're called penitentes (pen-ih-TEN-tays), named after people who march wearing tall, pointed hoods during a Spanish religious festival. The spikes get their jagged shape when snow skips the melting process and goes straight from a solid state to water vapor. This happens when the air is cold, but the sun's rays shine brightly upon the snow's surface.

COLOSSAL EXPERIMENT 2:
CRYSTAL BOWL

In our last experiment, you grew cubes of crystals. Now it's time to go even more colossal—as in a whole bowl of 'em! This is an experiment worth its salt!

CRYSTAL GROWTH METER

TIME UNTIL:
VISIBLE CHANGES: ONE HOUR
FINAL RESULTS: SIX HOURS

WHAT YOU'LL NEED

* 1/2 CUP (118 ML) HOT TAP WATER
* 1/2 CUP (170 G) EPSOM SALT
* SMALL GLASS BOWL
* SPOON
* REFRIGERATOR

BURN RISK:
Don't forget your adult helper!

WHAT YOU'LL DO

1. Pour the water and Epsom salt into the glass bowl.

2. Carefully stir the salt until it **dissolves**, being careful not to splash the hot water onto your skin. The salt will dissolve very slowly, so be patient, and take turns if your arm gets tired!

3. Put the bowl into the fridge, and check it after an hour. You should see some crystals growing in the solution.

4. Return the bowl to the fridge for a few more hours, checking it every now and then. When the experiment is done, spiky crystals will fill the whole bowl.

WHY IT WORKS

Hot water has more energy than cold water, and it can hold more dissolved material than cold water can. You can see proof of this as the water cools. It then begins to reject some of the Epsom salts. This process is called "coming out of the solution." The rejected particles bond together and form crystals as the water continues to cool.

Look really closely at your crystals. Do you remember how we learned crystals have different habits, or shapes? Crystals grown from Epsom salts have a needlelike habit. We bet you can see why!

NATURAL WONDERS

Magnesium, a key ingredient in Epsom salts, is also found in crystals in nature. One example is tourmaline, a gemstone that can grow to several pounds, or kilograms, in weight. The most unusual tourmaline gemstone has a name—the Great Divide—and was found in a Brazil mine in 2011. It gained fame for the pink streak of tourmaline that shoots out of its pink and blue base. The asking price for this rare find: $1.2 million. You may want to stick with Epsom salts!

COLOSSAL EXPERIMENT 3:
RAINBOW CRYSTALS

Are you ready to show off your science skills? It's time to make your masterpiece: a colorful crystal you can proudly show on your light-up display.

CRYSTAL GROWTH METER

BURN RISK:
Don't forget your adult helper!

TIME UNTIL:
VISIBLE CHANGES: ONE DAY
FINAL RESULTS: ONE WEEK

WHAT YOU'LL NEED

* 1 CUP (236 ML) WATER
* 2 PACKETS OF CRYSTAL-GROWING POWDER
* PLASTER CRYSTAL SEED
* SAUCEPAN
* SPOON
* PLASTIC MEASURING CUP
* FOOD COLORING (CHOOSE YOUR FAVORITE COLOR!)

WHAT YOU'LL DO

1. Ask your adult helper to heat the water on the stove until the mixture begins to simmer.

2. Stir the crystal-growing powder and food coloring into the water. Add food coloring. (Just a few drops will do!) Stir to combine.

3. Remove the pan from the heat, and let the mixture cool for about 15 minutes.

4. Ask your helper to pour the cooled solution into the plastic measuring cup.

5. Using the spoon, put the plaster crystal seed in the bottom of the cup.

6. Put the cup in a place where it will not be disturbed.

7. Check your results after a day. You should see crystals beginning to grow.

8. Carefully drain out any remaining liquid. Place the light-up cover over the cup. Now you're not just a scientist. You're an artist!

WHY IT WORKS

The powder—monoammonium phosphate, used in fertilizers and fire extinguishers—dissolves in the hot water into tiny **particles** you can't see with your naked eye. This creates what we call a **saturated** solution. Then, just like with the dissolved Epsom salts, the powder particles come out of solution and crystallize as the water cools.

NATURAL WONDERS

Like our crystal-growing powder, teeth and bones are made of a mineral that contains the element phosphorus. The mineral found in teeth and bones is called apatite. And the award for the scariest apatite-based animal with the largest appetite goes to the Tyrannosaurus rex, which stood at about 13 ft. (4 m) tall and 40 ft. (12.3 m) long. That makes for one truly colossal crystal skeleton!

COLOSSAL EXPERIMENT 4:
EGGSHELL GEODE

In nature, geodes can take thousands of years to form, but you can make one in just a few days using a few common kitchen items. Better yet, you can make it in your favorite color!

CRYSTAL GROWTH METER

TIME UNTIL:

VISIBLE CHANGES: 12 HOURS

FINAL RESULTS: ONE WEEK

WHAT YOU'LL NEED

* THREE LARGE EGGS

* PUSHPIN

* SMALL PAIR OF POINTED SCISSORS

* WHITE GLUE

* SMALL PAINTBRUSH

* SIX MICROWAVE-SAFE, WIDE-MOUTH GLASS JARS OR BOWLS

* 2 CUPS (473 ML) OF WATER

* 3/4 CUP (177 ML) ALUM POWDER (POTASSIUM SULFATE)

* FOOD COLORING

TIP: You can find alum powder in the spice section of your grocery store, or you can order it online.

WHAT YOU'LL DO

1. Carefully wash each egg, and make a hole in each end of each egg using a pushpin.

2. Holding an egg over a bowl, gently blow into the hole so the raw egg comes out on the other end.

3. Insert your scissors into a hole, and cut each shell in half lengthwise.

4. Gently wash the inside of the shells with soapy water (and your hands as well!). Pat the egg dry with a paper towel.

5. When the shells are completely dry, use a paintbrush to coat the inside of each shell with white glue on the inside of each shell.

6. Generously sprinkle alum powder over the wet glue. Let the shells dry overnight.

7. The next day, prepare the alum growing solution. In a glass jar or bowl, add the water. Ask an adult helper to heat water in the microwave until it is almost boiling, about one minute. Carefully pour the alum powder into the water, and stir until the alum powder has completely dissolved.

8. To make colored geodes, pour an equal amount of the water and alum powder mixture into each jar or bowl. Then add a different food coloring (or try a combination!) to each one. Stir each mixture with a spoon. Add more alum powder if the solution is watery. The solution should be saturated so that the water can hold as much alum powder as it can possibly hold.

9. Once the mixture is sufficiently saturated and the alum is completely dissolved, let the solution cool for about 30 minutes.

10. Carefully place one prepared eggshell in each of the colored growing solutions. Allow them to rest inside up at the bottom of the container. Make sure each eggshell is completely covered by the solution.

11. Set the container aside in a safe place overnight (or at least 12 hours) to allow the crystals to grow undisturbed. The longer the eggshells are in the solution, the larger the crystals will grow.

12. Carefully remove your finished geodes, and place them on a paper towel to dry.

Just like with our other materials, the alum can't stay dissolved as the water cools and evaporates, so the particles begin to crystallize on the inside of the eggshells. No waiting thousands of years for these geodes!

NATURAL WONDERS

Our homemade geodes may be a big deal, but the largest geode found in nature is a really big deal—big enough to host a crowd inside it! Workers discovered the Crystal Cave in Put-in-Bay, Ohio, in 1897 while digging a well for the winery above it. Many of the blue crystals were harvested to use in fireworks before the giant geode became a tourist attraction.

COLOSSAL EXPERIMENT 5:
ROCK CANDY

Rock candy is a crunchy crystal confection that will rock your taste buds! Who knew science could be delicious?

CRYSTAL GROWTH METER

TIME UNTIL:
VISIBLE CHANGES: ONE DAY
FINAL RESULTS: SEVEN DAYS

BURN RISK:
Don't forget your adult helper!

➤ WHAT YOU'LL NEED

* 1 CUP (236 ML) WATER

* 2 1/2 CUPS (500 G) SUGAR

* FOOD COLORING, IF DESIRED

* SAUCEPAN

* SPOON

* ONE CLEAR HEATPROOF GLASS JAR PER STICK OF ROCK CANDY

* WOODEN CRAFT STICKS OR LOLLIPOP STICKS

* ONE PLATE FOR EACH STICK USED

* SCISSORS

* DISPOSABLE PLASTIC LID (LIKE FROM A MARGARINE OR SOUR CREAM CONTAINER)

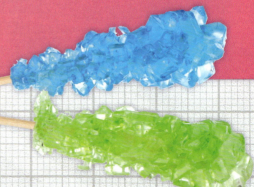

WHAT YOU'LL DO

1. Combine water and sugar in a saucepan.

2. Ask your adult helper to heat the mixture on the stove until it simmers.

3. Let it simmer for 30 minutes, stirring occasionally. Stir in food coloring, if desired.

4. Have your helper pour the mixture into the heatproof glass container.

5. Dip a wooden stick in the mixture, and set it on a plate to dry. Repeat with the remaining sticks, setting each one on a separate plate to speed the drying process. You're making **seed crystals**.

6. When the stick is dry, use scissors to poke a small hole in the middle of the plastic lid. Push the clean end of the craft stick up through the hole.

7. Set the lid on top of the glass container so the stick dangles in the liquid.

8. Check your rock candy's progress each day. You should see small crystals forming pretty quickly, but it may take a week or so for your sugary treat to finish growing. When the stick is covered with rocky chunks of sugar, it's time for dessert!

WHY IT WORKS

Just like with our other solutions, the dissolved sugar is forced out of solution as the liquid cools. The sugar particles cling to the seed crystals you made in Step 5 to create ever-growing sugar chunks. The longer you wait (and this requires patience!), the bigger your sugary treats will grow.

TIP: Treat yourself to a whole rainbow of colors by dividing the clear solution into several glass containers, and then add food coloring.

NATURAL WONDERS

Imagine your rock candy hanging from a cave ceiling or poking up from a cave floor, and you're picturing **stalactites** and **stalagmites**. Stalactites hang from cave ceilings, and stalagmites shoot up from cave floors. (To remember which is which, think "g" for ground and "c" for ceiling.)

The tallest stalagmite, found in Cuba, measures 220 ft. 6 in. (67.2 m), while the longest stalactite, found in Brazil, measures nearly 90 ft. (28 m).

COLOSSAL EXPERIMENT 6:
YOUR MOST COLOSSAL CRYSTAL YET

You've heard the expression that says, "Mighty oaks from little acorns grow." That means colossal things can grow from small seeds. Let's start with a crystal seed and see how big your crystal can grow!

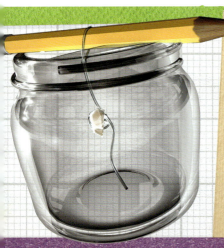

CRYSTAL GROWTH METER

TIME UNTIL:
VISIBLE CHANGES: SIX HOURS
FINAL RESULTS: THREE WEEKS

BURN RISK:
Don't forget your adult helper!

WHAT YOU'LL NEED

* HOT WATER
* ALUM
* DISPOSABLE CUP
* SPOON
* TWEEZERS
* 8-IN. (20-CM) PIECE OF FISHING LINE
* PENCIL
* HEATPROOF GLASS JAR

WHAT YOU'LL DO

1. Pour 2 tablespoons (30 ml) water and 1 teaspoon (5 g) alum into a disposable cup. Stir to dissolve.

2. Let the cup sit undisturbed for several days until all the water evaporates. You should see some alum crystals in the bottom of the cup.

3. It's time to make a seed crystal. Use the tweezers to pluck the biggest crystal out of the cup. Firmly tie a piece of fishing line around the crystal. Tie the other end of the line to a pencil. Leave about 6 in. (15.2 cm) of line between the crystal and the pencil.

4. Put ½ cup (118 ml) of hot water and 2 tablespoons (30 g) of alum into the heatproof jar. Stir to dissolve.

5. Lower the crystal you prepared in Step 3 into the jar. Rest the pencil across the top of the jar with the crystal dangling down. Twist the pencil to adjust the string so the crystal dangles in the center of the liquid.

6. Let the jar sit. Your crystal will grow for weeks or even months if you add fresh alum solution from time to time. Try to see how COLOSSAL your crystal can get!

WHY IT WORKS

Crystals like to gather in crowds! The particles connect with each other (or come out of solution) as the solution cools down. Your seed crystal attracted alum particles to it. Now instead of having one small seed crystal, you have one COLOSSAL crystal from all the alum particles crystallizing in the same spot.

NATURAL WONDERS

If you live in or visit New Mexico, you may want to visit Carlsbad Caverns, a system of about 80 caves filled with stalactites and stalagmites made of limestone. Scientists say a sea once covered the area, which has since become a desert. Over many years, water combined with an eat-through-your-skin acid slowly ate away at the limestone underneath to form the caves. But scientists didn't know how long the caves had been there—until they enlisted the help of alunite, an alum-based mineral found within the caves. By age-dating the alunite, they placed the age of the caves in the millions of years.

23

GLOSSARY

ATOM – the smallest unit of matter

CRYSTALLIZATION – the process that results in the formation of crystals

DISSOLVE – become part of a solution

ELEMENT – a substance found in nature that is in its simplest form

EVAPORATE – turn from liquid to gas or vapor

GEODE – a rock containing a crystal-filled cavity

GEOMETRIC – containing regular lines and shapes

HABIT – the shape of a crystal based on how it grows

MINERAL – a hard material that is found in nature and is not made of living things

MOLECULE – a group of atoms that join to form one unit

OPAQUE – not able to be seen through; not transparent

SATURATED – holding as much material as it can hold

SEED CRYSTAL – a crystal that acts as a growing surface for other crystals

SOLUTION – a liquid that contains a dissolved solid

STALACTITE – an icicle-like mineral deposit hanging from the ceiling of a cave

STALAGMITE – an icicle-like mineral growth rising from the floor of a cave

TRANSLUCENT – cloudy but allowing light to pass through

TRANSPARENT – clear and allowing light to pass through so things behind the transparent object can be seen clearly